Six Months Onboard

A Chapbook of Poetry

By

S.G. Williams

This is a work of creative fiction. Names, characters, places, and incidents either are the product of the author's imagination or are used fictitiously, and any resemblance to actual persons, living or dead, business establishments, events, or locales is entirely coincidental.

ISBN: 979-8-218-87429-2

For my Paisanos

The Poems

All poems herein were written between July 3rd 2025
and January 15th 2026 while working onboard a
well-known cruise ship in the Caribbean.

Ocean Traveling

Vast blue sheets with white foam

Spiderwebbed against the shimmering sea.

Paint the paths that I now roam

Alone, though never, captive and free.

Every breath and movement not my own

Apart from another who can see.

Only my mind hidden from other's souls.

Though not from mother ocean

Who's foamy web snare's controls

Of those caught in her motion.

'Ere long the horn blows,

And the spell breaks its notion.

S.G. Williams

Horizon Gazing

A thin line between sea and sky

Runs through my mind and across my eye.

It shows near and far, though never reached

As thirsting winds carry old lessons teached.

Oh Thesseuys never rests as the same winds blow

Across seas of time. As watered legends grow,

And span era and myth. Changed and yet the same.

A churning of salt, water, ancient ships claimed,

Within the great canvas renewed by and by in the tide.

That in sweet time relinquishes secrets beached,

To those who look out at horizon dawn's glow,

And like ancients think of tide and time tamed.

Port of Call

Salt wind on forward

Calm waters in the day's pier

Clouds cast the afternoon

Night Walks

Light fills the breezeway at night

A border drawn between ship and sea.

Man's made island casts bright,

Into the black world without beyond me.

Dawn orange life boats hang

As a barrier between me and water.

For their need the sea's not to blame,

They're if man's made land should falter.

Yet as I watch the moonless black,

Of sea and night.

How can I be sure she won't attack,

And show us her full might?

By sea's grace we sail

Across her expanse.

With a blowing gail,

Warning against foolish chance.

S.G. Williams

Rain on Water

Rain pin pricks the uneven surface
As I rock along in Tender.
Under hull waves move in wild circus
Without care for meter or measure.

Gentle winds chime the drops as we move
From ship to land,
And Tender rocks through wave's grooves.
Closed eyes hear nature's band.

Two Birds at Sea

Along early afternoon hulls
They lock wings and sore
Hungry and graceful gulls.
Down into the waves they tore.

Not a cloud to darken their way,
Only sun and swells and me.
Undeterred, even miles from any bay
The pair dances and dives free.

Tender Ride

Waking water waves

Behind our boat's bows

Past mild morning moorings

Countdown

Cogs of guarded logic crush

Vines of affections newly growing fruits.

As waves mark days in a rush

Till signing off leaves only mangled roots.

Life aboard does not pause,

As much as we may wish.

In such short a time what cause

Can cultivate lasting bliss?

S.G. Williams

Ever-After in Six Months

Don't linger in landside thoughts,

Things better grown in soil

Take no root in six month cots.

Even if a comfort amidst sailing's toil.

In man's made metal island

Nothing lasts in the ebb and flow of souls

Who work, earn, and live pile in.

Best smoother out the 'ever after' coals.

For what can grow so close so quick

Also survive the sudden tearing apart

By Gaia's ever flexing grip,

On one's sick for home heart?

Only hoped to reunite by corporate chance,

An unknown bureaucrat's whim to approve

Their request, given after a glance.

Lasting happiness given or taken as the papers move.

Serenity

Peaked speakers and clouds

Fill the open deck and sky.

Stars hide behind heaven's shrouds

I know they'll return by and by.

Though not soon enough to save in

Time, my eyes from the reflex to focus on

The display of cheap and craven

Desires, lonely hearts try to con.

Stars return, comfort me,

Chart course to what is sought.

From what is, in moment be,

To God's intended just aught.

<u>Have Not, Maybe Have</u>

Nothing can be mine while at sea,
Owned to all and none. The space
I fill only to work and to see
The sun rise another day. Escape,
In the smiles of others, who also
Claim naught but air.
They, like me, know all so
Well how this life strips you bare.

Tide rises and falls day
And day again. How long
Is it really mine to say
That this life holds any wrong.
Are those smiles content
In this abundant asceticism?
Is this greed I need repent
From masked self-centerism?

Six Months Onboard

Where in these holds

Do I claim to have a free

Me? A coldness of souls

That silently echo a joyous spree,

Shiver my mind. As I hope

To find a life of worth

Within this island secured by rope,

To the promise of a bountiful berth.

Rocky Crossing

Storm winds swell the sea's waves

As we rock along in worth-

Questionable cradle of luxury and work.

Lights of pleasures continue west,

Uncaring of Neptune's breath.

S.G. Williams

Routine

Four months with two ports,

Five days, five days, fours.

Over, over, over with sorts

That crave, not culture, only double pours.

Then two months, with three,

Thank the Lord for more.

Five, five, four, kill my glee

Of seeing the same moor.

Days, how many till I flee,

Left till I get to feel

Myself again and free.

How many, till I get to be real?

<u>Stillness</u>

In the lonely minutes
How do I fill my heart?
What need I do with it
Which might render me greater art?

Beauty to release my soul's coil,
From its lonely toil.

Between the coming and going
I watch the earth turn,
And the sea flowing.
Yet through it all my heart burns,
  Burns for more.

Oh Lord, will you show me?
How the moments passed
Through my fingers can be
The grains that solidify my soul's sand cast.

  I ask,
That this new mold, fills with a heart more bold.

S.G. Williams

<u>Echoes Past</u>

Spirits' of sailors past,

From these seas never passed.

In the nights I look for you,

      Who

Do not rest in boxes of oak or yew.

My eyes through shadows watch the sea

And strain to see.

Those who in their wool did dye

Themselves a shade against the fear to die.

In books young have read

      Tales

Yet never risked seeing the red

In eyes of men who won't feel sun

      Again

Or watch the years grow their son.

In them I watch for their

Coming, from here or there,

To know their souls for who they're.

Unworthy as I may be to even buy

My sailor's sparrow, yet hope to earn it bye and bye.

Land Longing

How does a heart at sea love?

Would it not be simpler to leave

It behind, and to simply shove

Aside all thought of gentle relief.

In its void hold the steel,

Hard as the vessel itself.

Be safe from what can feel

And sit your heart home on a shelf.

What do you do if you fail,

Fail to set aside caring?

If you set off down that trail

Of yearning for your heart's sharing.

Will the blood of life's nectar

Water fruitful trees in salt

Of sea? Amidst the bleak factor

That coming separation is neither's fault.

Roots will rip, as twined tree

On land, stretches longingly to flower

Of gulf. Strained, as such, we

Will need to swallow that pill ever sour.

Paisano

Short in stature

And in life large.

An unexpected teacher,

With knowledge to fill a barge.

Good, like the old boys,

Though not where they're usually found.

Quick to share simple joys,

And often in for a penny and the pound.

An Unexpected Answer

Heat, humid, sun,
Sat on the tender waiting.
Ideal thoughts turn to son,
Father, spirit, and praying.

Engine unmoving hums,
Crew and guests talk,
The heat drums,
All impede a practice I scoff,
      No more.

Careful ears listen, and hope
To hear anything
That could help me cope.
Sweet and light as the birds sing.

Nothing, as always.
Continue anyways.

Our Father begins in my mind,
Then the engine's movements start.
Soon the island is behind,
Our Father ends in my heart.

S.G. Williams

Escapism

Heart and habit at war

I want affection, attention, and care

Yet, my actions keep all outside my door.

While the years tack on gray strands to my hair.

Idol isolation arrives easily

To me. My life of watching

Others live drags on wearily,

Hard to hope of it changing.

As I medicate with mellow headphone

Songs of greater gained and lost love than mine.

Melodies that sooth and postpone

The active strike to end the lonely live-

      Feed of life.

<u>Adrift</u>

Am I a man of going,

Or coming from fear?

Will the heart of another longing

For me, justify every frustrated tear?

It remains to be seen if pining

Alone unmoors me from bitterness's pier.

Though I know the answer.

It doesn't make acceptance come faster.

An incubator of steel and toils

A drift on a course I didn't set.

What grows in the ship's mercurial soils?

Love of fear, or a fear of love let

Loose in the cabins and corridors unclaimed spoils.

Seas push and push my waters away from any outlet.

The swells of a hopeful soul crack my bitter hulls,

And my heart, from the wreak, truth pulls.

Bitter Bidding

Contract bids on the month's first
Give hope for a future made bright,
And wet once again the thirst
For a life of adventurous seas,
That over my mind cast its light.
Yet my say only extends to a click,
And a prayer that corporate sees
My request and approves.
Still I worry that I only trick
Myself. Will it truly be received well
By those who decide the moves
Of labours behind gracious masks?
I think only God can tell.
Until he graces me I wait,
And focus on my daily tasks.
Trust comes slow for his
Answer that will sate
The hunger anxiously wrought.
That burns beyond what is,
For what I wish to be aught.

Six Months Onboard

Unheroic

Pool balls crack on the felted table,
Full arms of instant noodles and waters
Fumble the door. I see it and am able
To aid, yet resolve through whiskey falters.

Others move, first one then
Another. To collect dropped undertaking,
My passive eyes watch like a hen
In a coop. A cage of my making.

I'm not the hero, quick to act.
How could I claim as much?
Drink laced thoughts make it a clear fact,
I don't leap to the rescue and such.

Flashes of the years past,
When I stood in silent inaction.
Like a stone too steadfast,
Yet lied myself into the helper's faction.

No, I stand by and watch,

The story of my life unfold.

There, but not meaning much,

And not kept in a place for those one dearly holds.

In my cabin again I try to rest,

With my mind awash in self affacing sorrow.

A sincere, I hope, promise to give the best,

When I open my eyes tomorrow.

The Enchantress

Enthralling songs a drift off the stage,

And she sweetly smiles in the Halls,

Mess, and Crew Bar. Her spell that cures age

Induced bitterness in myself and all.

Brown eyes which shine bright
As they catch the theater's light.
She weaves stories that delight,
And saves the spirit from aimless night.

How I'd bend, bleed, and break, to never make her,
The target of mine or any's, no matter how few,
Barb of world-sick bur,
Or vexing self-hexing fume.

Her joy's magic lights this floating iron caged world,
With a glow unfound when my own soul's unfurled.

Given from her is the sugar of life
Among the salt stained hulls of tired ship.
An antidote to the waves of strife,
That threaten to overtake the lip
Of my tired and hope-famished mind.
Care for tenderness not my own, makes bitter men kind.

Waves on Sand

Storm launched white swells crash

The sand, like soldiers of old.

Sea's endless battery of shore, finds

Resolve in high winds blown by ghosts past.

Landing craft of dead souls and sailors

Longing for life and land

Lap the sun stained wall of tide

And time, and retreat again

With no beach head.

Rain As We Cast Off

Gray tracks of sky's tears

Fall and haze the horizon.

Once the fuel but now the obscurer, of fears,

Only the immediate seen as I march on.

The gentle storm envelopes our way,

And I smell not the bleeding dirt

Of land. Only salt and damp out the bay.

As we fully put behind us the clay

Of home's shore that we skirt.

Only sea and rain stretch out for me.

What lingers in the waters ahead?

The future that I cannot see

Waits and on its hope my heart has fed.

Corporate Beaches

Week by week industry of paradise churns,

Turns, and wheels in poor sinners.

Who believe they can cut a slice of an Eden that burns

From Adam's reaping touch and carousel of foreigners.

Though paradise is not man's to make.

Cannot only God sow perfection in rock,

Soil, and tree? We sons of Eve only take,

And use. Still to these spoiled tropics we flock.

An escape from man made steel and glass

Blades that cut the heavens. Where we while

Away to grease the wheels of progress. Similarly crass

Macanations manicure these sands and island smiles.

Escape, no, only a change of masks.

Pencils pushed all the same

And the counters of beans check off their tasks.

I among them, with each check cashed, grow my shame.

Southern Comfort

25

Light and slight drawl,

Only onboard for two weeks,

Comforting as a shawl

Drawn tight. Not Northern, yet creeks

Along Minnesota woods wouldn't sound

As much like home as her voice.

Too soon to say good-bye,

Yet better before it spoils.

As my ruin with others came with a try

To better unwind the coils,

Each heart is defensively enshroud.

So for a moment at sea, in an echo of home, I rejoice.

S.G. Williams

<u>Night Before Sign-Offs</u>

Full moon caps apex of sky,

As thin clouds kaleidoscope paled light.

A perfect night to say good-bye

To Friends new yet old from ship life.

Cool air as we're still outside of port,

Provides canvas for the idle talk

Of social drink. Common in our sort

Who along the path of shared trial walk.

Tomorrow some leave and we remain

On the ship which cradles and strains.

Those who depart have with them obtained

What each of us wait to gain.

For tonight yet we are all the same:

Crew and friends. Under the watchful

Silver eye of heaven. Nothing needed to gain

In the pale glow. Heart's coffers found bountiful.

City-State of Friendliness

A city of friendly faces,

Yet how many may be held

In my heart as friend?

In the floating colony, to what end

Can I take these souls, and meld

With my life to fight with o'er years' paces?

When my own lips cruel in vain smile

Do I really mean it?

Maybe it's simply just easier

Than being honest about the pit

Formed round my tired heart. Perhaps the sleazier

Thing; either way I'm only here a short while.

Still these short lived connections

Remind me of the sweet nectar

I once tasted. When my heart knew

A kinship akin to Paris and Hector.

This floating city hardly echoes Troy. It's new

Not myth, and still filled with faint friendly reflections.

S.G. Williams

Prayers in Sunlight

Open deck in dawning day's sun,
Sits us three, tired, sore, and done.

Still waters hold us up in the bay
As to what each other considers, I cannot say.

Though we bow heads with hearts open and honest.
That seek to earn in ernest your promise.

Signed in innocence and sacrifice,
That frees us from crushing vice.

My back bathed in sunlight,
Contemplates the majesty of your might.

Fear forms wisdom of your love,
Yet my peaceful prince sends forth a dove.

Make me wise so that I my fear
The things that forsake the holy tears

You shed in sorrowing anguish so long ago.
In my heart show me my foe,

That I may take action against him.
A beast foul and filled past cruilitie's brim,

Or serpent still and plotting,
Or prideful despot marching and trotting

In vain display against our rightful king.
No, as I look I see the truth you bring,

No beast, dictator, or snake threatens me,
I am the one who keeps me unfree.

My sight of greatest good,
Blacked by the brim of my sin woven hood,

Hides the Father's face in the mirror.
Till Philia's light makes the image clearer.

Giving hearts lend strength to doff
The mask that prevents the holding a loft

Your name. Sun sweats my back
As we three sit and pray. Souls joined to act,

In the bounty of his gracious blessings
And from round my heart, replace sin soiled dressings.

S.G. Williams

Shoreleave

A bar where no one knows me,

Creates a simple pleasure.

It stills a heart that might rather flee,

From the isolating island, void of treasure.

For what riches can be gained in

This metal monster's belly?

When time tables mark every meeting

Tossing chance met thrills to the alley.

Routine, a numb familiarity festered

In every pore of the soul,

And fermented when sequestered.

Spreading till you're one of the fold.

Cold beer on the lips,

Washes away the rot

Revel in its foamy kiss,

And know time will change your lot.

Churning Dreams

Torn dreams spill out

Like upset waters following the aft.

Eventually the echoes of their blissful shouts

Fade from ship sail filling gale to humble draft.

Gone to the tide and those

Fancies once clutched to so tight.

With this flight a new world is posed

To tempt me to assert my right.

Could I take the rigging like times ago

When arm's strength and will carried

You forward? I'm a sort to forgo

The joys of dirt, and let I be whim ferried.

Though is it the flighting fancies of my heart

That guides purpose? I hope to know before my ships

      depart.

Shout-Outs

Cards for free coffee

The thank you for my efforts.

Do I deserve them?

What else would I need

To be happy to receive

Gratitude from them?

I wish that I knew

What my own heart requires

To feel like enough.

Six Months Onboard

<u>What's Returned to Sea</u>

Tender weighed down with goods

Casts off from mother vessel.

Heavy with the day's drinks and foods.

As the morning sun casts off Calypso's skin

It glows a radiance sparking blood to swell

And alights the soul to quicken.

The beauty of goddess sea unblemished by fin

Casts out to smooth horizon.

Till I turn my head to see her stricken

By iron stud of pleasure seekers wrought.

Its crude shadow blocks warming sun

From growing the rose to her cheeks.

Instead she must chew the rot

Trailed by mechanical wasting.

I know well how violently it reeks,

From the galley's waste and I wish,

For her to be given from us better tastings.

Tender rocks and I whisper silent contritions

For the left over waste we feed her fish.

The light off her form might be her peace with conditions.

S.G. Williams

Longing, Not Lusting

Tide breaks 'gainst the sorrow hearted hull

And my caged imagination fills the cracks.

Shining as it culls

Sense and reason like scourges cross backs.

Flesh stripped clean to heart

In its rightful cage

Of bone. It prys bars apart

Uncaring of pain in its loving rage.

Not that it loves true.

It lusts for what's not.

A life of tenderness away from the rue

Suffering seas; a warmed bed, not a cot.

A faithful heat never known,

And not yet given in His time.

First, unlearn that it's a possession to own,

Then, see it comes when gifted to be me and mine.

The Calling

Begotten in my soul is a thrist

For the immaterial spring of knowing.

It bubbles just beyond that first

Line of horizon; tasted in salt wind blowing.

Alight upon deck and hull,

I drink deep that ever retreating line.

My companions the cloud and gull

Linger along under a morning shine.

Haze of face in reflected light

Bleeds out the calling.

A promise to make ribs tight

Around heart. Beauty forces tears' falling.

In day my heart's missing piece clear.

Adventure for more drives me,

To hide from the fear.

That I truly and desperately need thee.

A love that cannot be held in hands,
Or embraced in body's arms.
With it I'll never exchange bands,
Or even small lovers' charms.

Yet without I'll never end my quest,
My thirst will never be sated.
Be it travels worst or best,
Without Greatest I'm misery fated.

My eyes to horizon cannot see,
That the grail most desperately sought
Already resides within me.
Waiting, filled, with your love brought.

A Dead Bird on the Deck

Still feathers on small body
Resting, not sleeping, on the breezeway.
Music and chatter drifting from the lobby
Unknowing and uncaring of you who lay.

Would you be gone if we didn't sail?
Could your song still chirp merrily,
Or nest you through tropical gale?
Why not you from this unsteady and ferrous perch flee?

Did I ever hear your song,
Or were they cries of terror,
As we took you to the sea's throng
And journey away from harbor?

Music will still play, and laugher shared,
As we ferry vacationers along.
You will not know, how little they cared,
For your cries for home disguised as birdsong.

How can I shuttle you to rest?

On this mass of metal no peace exists,

I'm sorry it's here stillness comes to your breast.

More so in a place where hands are bound by inept wrists.

So there you are, dead on the breezeway.

As we clip along warm waters.

My eyes look back at vanishing bay,

And pray for the victims of our travel's slaughters.

A Doctor Who Paints and Shares Chocolate

Hands that heal color the page

With brush and pallette vivid.

Strokes against the white assuage

Worries, and cares of patients calm and livid.

Hands that heal bare the weight

Of a world not always kind.

Even so, they have strength to gently wait

Out the arrow or sling with patient mind.

Hands that heal hold together a ship

When blood is in need,

Feet on stairways slip,

And unseen tears need a hopeful seed.

Hands that heal offer chocolate dark,

To mend not only body but spirit.

A simple sign of caring matriarch

Who acts out the good of doctor's writ.

What to her can I offer in return?

Apart from earnest yearnings to see her worries burn.

Silence until she from the growing paints look,

And shows the lemon image on her sketchbook.

Even in her rest beauty drips from her finger's

Tips, and upon my heart care lingers.

Don't disturb hand that heal

When they paint.

Hands that prove God's love real

Know healing is an art, and art is healing to a saint.

My Return

When I leave this faux island

Will I be the one to return?

As salt spray, wet air, and

Toil-bound hearts continue to burn

In their perpetual voyage.

What of me will remain

On that steel sea splitting vessel?

Steps down the gangway may reclaim

A life atop dirt and tar where I wrestle

To face the day with courage.

When I've tasted the burning fuel,

Wind whipped grains of sand,

Transitory bliss; gently cruel.

Is it I that will feel the grass and

Trees, or will my soul remain in steerage?

The sea claims her due from a man,
As sailors of ages hence claim
Slivers of my soul. What can,
Must, be done for me to remain
On course in my life's voyage?

Once more cast to the swells
Of a life trotting along paths
Laid out in cruel parallels,
And webbing forks. My line casts
Out to fill the holds of my will's steerage.

Aboard kind words, faces, and hearts
Saw me through the months, days,
And lonely hours. They made the charts
My tired soul could plot to hopeful bays
Where had been waiting treasure: a new life's courage.

S.G. Williams is a Minnesota native who's spent the better part of his adult life bouncing around from the Twin Cities, to Ireland, St. Louis, and a variety of other shorter stops in a partially nomadic life. A jack of all trades dipping his toes in the worlds of hospitality, security, live entertainment, manufacturing, retail, and finance; he's setting out to share some of those experiences through his writings.

You can follow his adventures and get updates on his future publications here:

Instagram: @hemingwayknockoff